THE
PARTING

To Jeri—
Thanks for your
help.
Karen Morderan
3/22/94

THE
PARTING

~

KAREN MODEROW

JordanWest
PUBLICATIONS

Jordan West Publications
Alpharetta, Georgia

First printing, January 1996
Library of Congress Catalog Card Number 95-60950
ISBN 0-9643189-0-3 (pbk)

Published by Jordan West Publications
Building B-9, Suite 547
2880 Holcomb Bridge Road
Alpharetta, Georgia   30202

Printed in the United States of America.

In memory of my grandfather,
Hiram Thomas Westbrook

Acknowledgments

I am grateful to my friends who generously offered their time to evaluate and proof this book: Linda O'Kay, David Buzzy, Steve Alper, Suzanne Haley, Jeri Terkosky, Marla Chambless and Sharon Theis.

Also my deepest love and appreciation goes to those special people who encouraged me along the way—David Perry, Elizabeth DeBeasi, my sister, Sharon Brookshire and especially, my husband, Joseph.

Table of Contents

Introduction 11

Part One: Facing Death
   1. Saying Good-bye 17
   2. Dealing with Ambivalence 21

Part Two: Defining The Life Of A Loved One
   3. Character Traits 33
   4. Biographical and Personality Questions 41

Part Three: Planning The Service
   5. Elements of the Service 51
   6. Who Does What? 55

Part Four: Creative Celebrations Of Life
   7. Creative Eulogies, Rituals, and Symbols 63
   8. Music 71

Part Five: Writing It Down
   9. Memorial Service Checklist 81
  10. Memorial Service Planner and Bulletin 85

Part Six: Planning Your Own Service
  11. Participating in Your Parting 93

     A Note From the Author 97
     Resources 101

Introduction

Death is always a delicate subject. No matter how we phrase it, we are often uncomfortable discussing our own death or that of our loved ones. Perhaps we fear that planning somehow hastens the day. But when death intrudes, most of us wrestle to find some meaning and purpose in it. We want to redeem the situation—to not let death have the last word.

The Parting is written with three readers in mind: the person who will be planning the funeral of a loved one; the person who is called upon to participate in such a service (perhaps a minister or counselor); and the person who wishes to plan his own memorial service.

A word of caution is in order for those acting as a facilitator for the family: Use discernment as to whether it's appropriate to work directly from this book in planning the memorial service. The family may be in shock after a death, especially if it was sudden and a fill-in-the-blank form may be perceived as an affront to their grief. Remember that the primary purpose for the questions, lists, and forms is to help the family work through the grieving process—to help them define and celebrate the one they mourn. It may be better to use the book as a guide and to ask some of the more pertinent questions in the course of your normal conversation with the family.

Those who have had the opportunity to prepare emotionally for the death of a loved one, and those who themselves have come to terms with the reality of death, will be most open to participating in this process. However, every situation is unique and each person is different. Even in the same family, responses to death can vary greatly. The one leading the family through the journey of parting will be most effective if he or she remains flexible and makes a priority of meeting the needs of those who are hurting.

The process of planning a funeral may be most wrenching to those who face impending death. It's hard to think of ourselves or our loved ones in the past tense. Were it not for the conviction that participating in the formal parting is important, it would be a cruel exercise, yet perhaps it will encourage you to know that most who have gone through the process agree that the benefits far outweigh the pain.

One mother whose teenage son has muscular dystrophy said, "At first, I did not want to do this—all I could think of was how hard it would be. I wanted to think positively about Grant's life, not plan for his death, but once I got into the process I couldn't believe how therapeutic it was."

When it came to getting things down on paper, she discovered Grant had some very strong opinions. "Because I know him so well I thought I knew what he would want at his funeral. I was shocked to find out how clueless I was." She learned that Grant wants the graveside service first, then a celebrative service in the church. He also wants lots of singing led by a contemporary band made up of his friends. "I don't know how I'll feel when the day actually comes," his mother said. "In the meantime, it's a great relief to know the plans are in the drawer. If I want to change something then, I can, but if I don't want to, the work is done and what we've planned already has meaning for us."

Whether the funeral is planned before or at the time of death, *The Parting* can walk you through this important task. It's not necessarily a book to be read from cover to cover. You may want to do a quick overview and choose those aspects you feel ready to handle. Some sections you may want to come back to. Others may have no appeal at all. Give yourself the freedom to explore the process. See how you feel about it. And expect some resistance. If planning your own funeral or that of a loved were easy, there would be little need for a book like this one. But as we'll see, the process offers tremendous benefits.

The Parting will help the reader organize a funeral service that will minister to the deep emotional and spiritual needs of family and friends. But though it provides a format to start the planning process, the ultimate goal is to get past the form and into the creative realm.

Throughout the book, I will use the terms *funeral* and *memorial service* interchangeably, even though *memorial service* may imply that the body is not present. *The Parting* deals specifically with the service. Regardless of what form of burial is chosen, this memorial is the focus of the book.

While *The Parting* can be used by the reader to plan his own memorial service, for the sake of simplicity, I have written all but the last section from the viewpoint of one who is planning a funeral for another person.

Lastly, this book is written from a Christian perspective. Being a Christian, it is impossible for me to write positively about death from any other. Yet whether or not the reader shares my beliefs, there is much from *The Parting* that can be applied. We are all unique individuals, who, upon passing this life, deserve a personal and meaningful farewell.

However, I would be dishonest to attempt to write this book without a clear statement of my faith in God and the hope I have in Him of eternal life. It colors my view of death and is my primary motivation for writing this book. I believe that in death, as in life, we should honor God. The way we deal with death can be an effective witness to the faithfulness and goodness of God. It's an opportunity we shouldn't miss.

It is my desire that *The Parting* will inspire the reader to creatively participate in a process that will bring encouragement, comfort, and hope to those who grieve.

∽

Part One:

Facing Death

∽

For I am persuaded that neither death nor life,
nor angels nor principalities nor powers,
nor things present nor things to come,
nor height nor depth nor any other created thing,
shall be able to separate us from
the love of God which is in Christ Jesus our Lord.

—Romans 8: 38–39

Chapter One

Saying Goodbye

I struggled to keep my attention on the minister as he gave the eulogy for my grandfather. I wasn't distracted—I was disturbed. The man being described bore little resemblance to the man I knew as Granddad. It seemed odd that at his death, he was practically canonized for character traits he seldom showed in life. The real tragedy was that there was so much about his personality and earthly journey that was worthy of praise.

Granddad was nine when his father died. His mother, unable to cope, was committed to a mental institution where she died years later. Granddad and his brothers were farmed out to various relatives who hired them out, took the money they earned, and subjected them to severe emotional and physical abuse. In desperation, my grandfather ran away. At twelve, he was literally alone in the world with no resources other than his willingness to work hard.

Somehow, he survived. And when he married and had children, Granddad determined to give his boys a better life than he'd had. Out of the ashes of his own violent past, he struggled to raise a family. Because of his background, he could seldom give or receive love. All he had to pass on to his boys were the qualities that had allowed him to survive—hard work, perseverance, diligence, and honesty.

Granddad felt a great responsibility to send his boys into the world better prepared than he had been. "The one thing I want you to have is an education," he told them. "No one can ever take that away from you."

At Granddad's funeral, three sons stood as testimony to his determination and sacrifice: a dentist, a minister, and a doctor. I know he was proud of them, though I never heard him say so. And I was proud of my grandfather. Only once did he talk to me about his past. In the nursing home shortly before his death, his eyes filled with tears as he spoke of his brothers and the hard life they lived. It was the only time I ever saw him cry.

How much he had overcome! And how grateful I was for the strength of his character that enabled him to persevere in the worst of circumstances. I recognized that I, too, benefited from the better life he had given my father.

As the service continued, I grieved for Granddad. I grieved for the loneliness and isolation of his life, for the opportunities I had missed to know more of him. And I wished for a more fitting tribute at his death.

After his funeral, I felt as though the last chapter of his life's book had been omitted. I wanted his passing to be noted by something more than a generic eulogy. I wondered what we could have done to make it different. And why did it matter?

At that moment, I realized the importance of the parting. Whether a loved one is being cremated or buried, whether his service is to be public or private, religious or nonreligious, the family and friends left behind participate in some ritual of parting. That ritual can be a rote performance of duties as the family members move through a fog of details pertaining to the funeral, or it can be a creative celebration that will honor the deceased and bring comfort to the living.

It *does* matter how we say good-bye. Something within us longs for a fitting conclusion to our relationship with a loved one. Yet if the memorial is unsatisfactory, it seldom is because of callousness, but because we're unprepared or don't know what to say or do.

Making burial arrangements in advance is a concept that has become increasingly prevalent in the past few years. It seems fitting that as we make preparation for the physical body, we should also prepare for our spiritual and emotional parting. I hope this book will encourage you to do that. Though it provides step-by-step directions for planning a funeral, it should also be a springboard for creativity.

What is it we hope to accomplish through the memorial service? There are usually deep psychological and spiritual needs we seek to satisfy when we experience the loss of a loved one; the memorial service can and should address these needs. A meaningful parting should give one the opportunity:

- ∽ To celebrate the life of the deceased.
- ∽ To express grief through planning of the service.

- ∞ To acknowledge and affirm a realistic view of the loved one.
- ∞ To promote reconciliation with estranged family or friends.
- ∞ To worship God and invoke His strength and comfort.

In the following chapters, we'll explore how this can be done.

Chapter Two

Dealing
with Ambivalence

Carol and JoAnne were teenagers when they discovered they were step-sisters. Their father, Sam, had two families—one in New York and one in Connecticut. He split his time between them and for years, neither knew the other existed. The children in both families coped as best they could when the truth became known. In time, both wives left him. Then Sam lost his eyesight and found himself dependent upon the very people he had hurt and betrayed. His children, then married with families of their own, took him in as his health began to deteriorate.

"At first, it was hard to deal with him being sick," said JoAnne. "I had been living with bitterness and rejection for so long that I resented having to do more. When he got so bad that we started looking for a nursing home, he offered Carol $50,000 to buy a house so he could live with her. It was out of the question—he needed care around the clock. But it hurt me that in the six years my father lived with me, he had many opportunities to help financially when we really needed it, and he never would."

Carol said, "I was angry with my dad because he took away a relationship I deserved as a child. He cared only about himself. Whenever I visited him, we always had a confrontation. I was never good enough. Never loved him enough. No matter what I gave, he wanted more."

The dementia Sam suffered in his last two years made him even more demanding and unreasonable. Carol and JoAnne struggled with anger even though both sincerely tried to offer forgiveness. His death left them with unexpected emotions.

JoAnne said, "I felt compassion for him and that surprised me. He really suffered. I remember thinking, Thank God, it's all over. I was glad he was out of his misery."

Carol's reaction was quite different. "I missed him and I couldn't understand it. When he was alive, I didn't want to be with him. It was burden off me when he died, but there was still this great emptiness. I guess it was realizing that now things could never be the way I hoped they would be."

Conflicting Emotions

Carol and JoAnne's story may be extreme, but it illustrates a universal principle: One of the most stressful aspects of facing death is that it releases a torrent of conflicting emotions. At first, we may be overwhelmed by gratitude for what the loved one meant in our lives. Joy may surprise us as we reminisce of good times. A sweet awareness of life's fragility may give us a heightened appreciation for others we love. Then guilt, regret, and anger can come in like a flood. The defenses we have used throughout our lifetime to deny these emotions can be shattered by the reality that our earthly relationship with that person is over.

Most of us are very adept at blocking out any emotions that are inconsistent with the way we view ourselves and our families, be they positive or negative. But if ever we are inclined to look for a true, honest appraisal of a loved one and our relationship to him or her, it is when we come face-to-face with death. Its brutal assault to our ordered world gouges out a vulnerability seldom experienced in any other context. At that point, we can choose one of several responses: We can deny the conflict, we can allow guilt to consume us, or we can commit ourselves to a process of accepting the reality of who our loved one was and what we meant in each other's lives.

Abandonment

After having an angioplasty, Ada's husband recovered well physically, but he withdrew, refusing to eat, to open his eyes, or to talk with family members. A few weeks later, he died. Ada said, "I still feel so angry with him. He knew he was slipping mentally, and he was scared." Her voice trailed off as she stared blankly into space. "I know he didn't want to live like that," she added softly, "but we were married 31 years, and he just left me alone."

Such feelings of abandonment are not uncommon, especially if the loved one made choices that contributed to his or her death. If factors like suicide, reckless behavior, or an unhealthy lifestyle were involved, that sense of having been willfully deserted is greatly intensified. The same is true if we were denied the opportunity to say or do what we wanted to before the death. One of my dearest friends often expressed her fear of becoming a burden to others. When she became terminally ill, she checked herself into a care-taking facility and refused to see her closest friends or family. It was agony for those who loved her. We couldn't believe that someone who had been there for us at every critical juncture of our lives would leave us a moment before she had to. And when she did, we felt very much abandoned.

No one lives or dies to himself, no matter how much we'd like to think otherwise. And sometimes those we love make choices about their dying that make it harder for us. Unfortunately, we can't rewrite the ending, but we can come to terms with the reality by providing our own closure to their deaths. The most obvious and beneficial way to begin, is by actively participating in the memorial service. Why? Because the social expectation of a funeral encourages us to find and express some purpose and understanding of our loved one's life and death. And the very process that helps us define the qualities of the deceased and celebrate them in a service will help us come to terms with many of our feelings, including abandonment.

It needs to be said that the death of anyone who is close to us, to some degree, feels like abandonment. In a sense their death throws us into our own life-death struggle to survive. This is especially true for dependents, children and spouses, who recognize at a gut level that whatever security they received from their loved one is forever gone. Not only is there an emotional amputation, our physical and finan-cial security may be severed as well. When we feel least able to do so, we're forced to make life-changing decisions, and the common response to the pressure is to blame the one who has left us in that precarious place.

This creates a painful paradox. At the very time we are most aware of how much we loved someone, we may also feel totally abandoned by them. It's important to recognize this conflict because it does a lot to explain our vacillating emotions. If unaware, we may spend a tremendous amount of energy trying to sublimate the negative emotions—energy needed to cope with the difficult days ahead. If instead, while understanding and honoring our loved one, we accept the ambilavence, we'll be taking the first steps toward resolving some of these issues.

Regrets

My mother was 39 when she died of cancer. During her long illness, I maintained things on the home front while attending college nearby. Though I did all I could to meet her physical needs, I felt guilty that we seldom connected emotionally about her death. Some instinct told me we needed to, but being only 19 myself, I was afraid of saying or doing the wrong thing. So I waited for her to offer something that would open the door. I wanted a blessing or some acknowledgment of what awaited us. But it never came.

Now, as a mother myself, I can appreciate the anguish she must have felt in leaving three children behind. How I wish I'd been wiser. If only I'd known then what I know now—that there is value in honest communication no matter how painful the subject. But I said nothing, she said nothing, and then she died. To this day, I feel the loss of what her words could have meant to us.

The hope of eternal life comforted me in the loss of my mother, but a "sting" of death remained in the sorrow of my regrets. Long after the raw pain of her death subsided, I was tortured by them. Why didn't we give each other the emotional support we both needed? Why didn't I ask for her blessing? Why didn't she offer it?

This painful experience taught me that even in our most nurturing and uplifting relationships, the finality of death confronts any conflict in our hearts. Though psychologists agree that sublimating the negative aspects of our relationships is detrimental to our emotional well being, the emotional shock of death often leaves us unable to respond to reality in the healthiest way. We may feel a strong need to express our anguish, yet experience an equally compelling need to deny anything that might darken our rose colored glasses. What is needed is a forum that will help identify conflicts and put them in perspective. And that's the opportunity the parting offers us.

As my family and I went through this process for my mother's funeral, seeds were planted that helped me come to terms with my regrets. My mother struggled with deep feelings of inferiority. With only a high school education, speaking and writing were especially torturous for her. She wasn't big on symbols or ceremonies...she just was. When she was living, that was enough. But when she died, I longed for some tangible evidence that she had loved me— a letter, a verbal statement of what we meant to each other, perhaps a parting gift. I wanted physical documentation of our precious relationship.

Exploring my mother's life affirmed to me that her strength was simply her presence. Though she herself was quiet and very shy, she had a dynamic way of relating one-on-one. It was probably her selflessness. Her gift was making the other person shine. She did it without grand gestures and with very few words. Once I asked, "If one word could describe you, what would you like it to be?" She replied, "Kind. I would like to be known as being kind." Her answer stunned me. It's the last quality to which I would've thought to aspire.

And she was kind yet also full of fun. She had a quirky little smile and liquid brown eyes. One of her little nephews once said, "Aunt Atha, you look like a baby cow...smiling." That certainly was an unusual description, but somehow it did capture the gentleness of her personality.

In time, I accepted that what I wanted from my mother before she died was unrealistic, given who she was. It was not her nature to think in terms of imparting a blessing or initiating a symbolic gesture. Had I thought to ask for a formal blessing, she'd gladly have given it, but it wasn't her way. Instead, she blessed me every day in the way she loved me.

After my mother's death, friends and family gathered at our home. For hours on end we raised our questions, wept over our loss, and returned over and over again to the force of her personality and what she meant in our lives. It was an invaluable process. Because of my grief, only part of it could be absorbed, yet later, as I was emotionally able to handle it, I drew on what I heard at that time.

Perhaps the most common regret felt by those who grieve for a loved one is remorse for taking him for granted. We fail to appreciate that which is most readily available to us. Often, it is not until we lose someone that his real value to us becomes painfully evident.

Maybe we could've done something different yet chose not to. Then we need to remember that freedom from guilt requires inner healing and where there is sin, the forgiveness of God. It's unlikely that deep emotions will be transformed through any one act, but the memorial service can be a step in the right direction.

Making the service an honest reflection of our loved one's life often gives us the perspective and understanding needed for our own healing. Sometimes just participating in a final ritual of parting provides the cathartic release of emotions that allows us to forgive ourselves for unfinished things that haunt us.

Anger and Frustration

In creating a unique memorial service, one objective is to find those things that are legitimately praiseworthy about the one who has died, and to express them in a way that would honor him or her. For those who have left a trail of goodwill, encouragement, and laughter, this is easy. But what about those whose difficult personalities created havoc wherever they went? There are those who abandoned and abused their loved ones, and those who were unable to rise above alcohol or drug addictions to be good parents or spouses. What do you say about these people when the emotions felt by their families range from a desperate love to anger, perhaps even hate?

Such ambivalence is often why the family chooses a generic service. It allows us to gloss over reality—to lie to ourselves and to others. It may smooth the waters long enough to conduct a burial, but denying the truth ultimately works against healing and provides no opportunity for us to come to terms with the contradictory emotions stirred by the loss.

My husband faced this dilemma when his father died. After a bitter divorce, Joe's father, Clarence, broke all relationships with his family. Twenty-four years later, a police officer informed Joe of his father's sudden death. It seemed ironic that Joe, who had been sixteen the last time he saw or spoke to his father, could legally be Clarence's next of kin.

As Joe made funeral arrangements, he struggled with what to say for his father's eulogy. Since none of the family even knew who Clarence's friends were, Joe couldn't ask them to participate. The family announced the date and time of the memorial service in the local paper and hoped that anyone who would want to attend would see it.

Steps Toward Healing

Though Joe knew it would be best to accept his dad as he was and to forgive him, he found it wasn't that easy. While his father lived, Joe successfully consigned his father to his subconscious. Death, however, dredged up hurts of childhood that could not be dismissed. There was no way he could absorb the impact of those lost years in a few days.

However, he did make some choices that allowed him to face his relationship with his dad honestly.

First, at the funeral, he stated, "My father was a very complex man." Joe acknowledged his own inability to understand why this intelligent, gifted man died estranged from every member of his family. The small chapel was filled with people who came to show their respects to Clarence. Several spoke to Joe afterward and confirmed that they shared his perplexity. "You're right," said a man who had worked beside Clarence for thirty years, "I was probably Clarence's closest friend, and I never understood him." Joe's eulogy for his father set the tone for that kind of honesty. It allowed for both truth and mercy, and both were needed for family and friends to come to terms with the circumstances.

The second choice Joe made which helped him overcome his bitterness toward his father was to focus on the good that was evident in Clarence's life and personality. Philippians 4:8 says, "whatever things are true, whatever things are noble, whatever things are just, whatever things are pure, whatever things are lovely, whatever things are of good report, if there is any virtue and if there is anything praiseworthy—meditate on these things." (NKJV) Everyone has something praiseworthy about them. And the more difficult the personality, the more important it is to go through a process that will help us focus on that good.

Joe's father was a man of character and conviction, known for his honesty and dedication to a job well done. The fact that he could show little kindness to his family was a sad commentary on his troubled life. He was a man to be pitied. Understanding that, Joe could speak well of his father at the funeral, and still express his inner anguish at the loss of relationship.

Making Peace

Even in the best of circumstances, most of us have some regrets about the important relationships in our lives. We wish we had been more sensitive, more expressive, less selfish, more loving. Whatever our concern, as we participate in the parting, it's important to make peace with ourselves and with God. As much as possible, we should allow the planning and execution of the memorial service to be a balm that will aid the healing process.

Those who are closest to the deceased should also be aware of their power to impart forgiveness on behalf of the deceased to others. Family members as well as the minister need to be aware if there will be those in the congregation who should be given special consideration.

At one funeral, a minister spoke directly to the children of a young man who had died. In the eulogy he conveyed the deep love and concern the dying father had expressed for them. It was a beautiful gesture that was no doubt very meaningful to the children who were addressed, but the minister was unaware that sitting right beside them were the man's two children from a former marriage. There was no animosity between the two families, but the oversight caused needless pain for two hurting children who had been inadvertently ignored.

The family should be especially sensitive to situations such as this, and avoid saying or doing anything within the service that would inflict pain on someone else. As much as possible, the immediate family should use the memorial service as an opportunity to facilitate healing not only for themselves, but for others.

Where do we begin? How can we hope to give perspective to complex relationships, to condense the dynamics of a lifetime into one service? The place to start is by attempting to verbalize those qualities that characterized the loved one.

᪢

Part Two:

Defining the Life of a Loved One

᪢

A man is valued by what others say of him.

—Proverbs 27:21

Chapter Three

Character Traits

*U*nconsciously, *most of us evalu-
ate our friends and family in terms of their character, and
relate to them accordingly. We go to certain friends when we
are hurting, because we know they are good listeners or will
give wise counsel. We call on those who have a contagious
enthusiasm for life when we want to have fun. When we
need support, we know who can be counted on to be generous
and forgiving. Analytical friends may seem overly critical*

when we're insecure, but we seek them out when we need inspiration to achieve our best.

It seems appropriate then, to bring this unconscious process into our consciousness as we prepare for the parting. We can gain a better perspective of our loved one's life and his value to us as we consider who he really was. To get a balanced view, it may be helpful if more than one family member participates in this process.

The following list is by no means comprehensive, but I hope it will help you key in on specific traits that characterize your loved one. It may bring to mind other traits not mentioned here. As you skim through the list, check off those qualities that best describe him. Afterward, go back and further clarify in your mind what were integral parts of his personality.

Please note that after the positive trait, a less desirable trait is mentioned. Considering each quality in the light of its opposite should provide a clearer picture of what the positive character trait entails. (I am grateful to Youth With A Mission for their contribution to this section.)

Character Traits

∾ *Alertness vs. Unawareness*
Being able to anticipate right responses to that which is taking place around you.

∾ *Attentiveness vs. Unconcern*
Exercising your senses to perceive the true spirit and emotions of those around you.

∾ *Availability vs. Self-centeredness*
Making your own schedules and priorities secondary to others'.

∽ *Boldness vs. Fearfulness*
Being confident that what you have to say or do will result in lasting benefit.

∽ *Cautiousness vs. Rashness*
Knowing how important right timing is in accomplishing right actions.

∽ *Compassion vs. Indifference*
Investing whatever is necessary to heal the hurts of others.

∽ *Contentment vs. Covetousness*
Being satisfied with what you have.

∽ *Creativity vs. Underachievement*
Approaching a need, a task, or an idea from a fresh perspective.

∽ *Decisiveness vs. Doublemindedness*
Being able to finalize difficult decisions.

∽ *Deference vs. Rudeness*
Limiting your freedom in order not to offend the tastes of others.

∽ *Dependability vs. Inconsistency*
Fulfilling what you consented to do even if it means unexpected sacrifice.

∽ *Determination vs. Faint-heartedness*
Purposing to accomplish goals regardless of the opposition.

∽ *Diligence vs. Slothfulness*
Using whatever energy and resources are required to complete a task.

∞ **Discernment vs. Judgment**
Seeing through a surface problem to root causes.

∞ **Endurance vs. Giving Up**
Possessing the inward strength to withstand stress and accomplish a worthwhile goal.

∞ **Enthusiasm vs. Apathy**
Expressing with your spirit the joy of your soul.

∞ **Fairness vs. Partiality**
Looking at a situation from the viewpoint of each person involved.

∞ **Faith vs. Presumption**
Visualizing what God intends to do in a given situation and acting in harmony with it.

∞ **Flexibility vs. Resistance**
Being willing to compromise when appropriate.

∞ **Generosity vs. Stinginess**
Being willing to share your resources to meet the needs of others.

∞ **Gentleness vs. Harshness**
Expressing personal care appropriate to another's emotional need.

∞ **Gratefulness vs. Unthankfulness**
Acknowledging the benefits brought to your life by others.

∞ **Humility vs. Pride**
Recognizing that God and others are actually responsible for the achievements in your life.

∞ *Initiative vs. Unresponsiveness*
Recognizing and doing what needs to be done
before being asked to do it.

∞ *Joyfulness vs. Self-pity*
Allowing the delights of life to overwhelm hardship
and adversity.

∞ *Kindness vs. Maliciousness*
Exhibiting gentleness and compassion toward others.

∞ *Loyalty vs. Unfaithfulness*
Maintaining commitments made to people, beliefs,
and ideals.

∞ *Meekness vs. Anger*
Being willing to endure injury with patience and
without resentment.

∞ *Obedience vs. Willfulness*
Being free to be creative under the protection of
divinely appointed authority.

∞ *Orderliness vs. Disorganization*
Preparing yourself and your surroundings to
achieve the greatest efficiency.

∞ *Patience vs. Restlessness*
Being willing to wait without complaint or anxiety
for the resolution of a difficult or adverse
circumstance.

∞ *Resourcefulness vs. Wastefulness*
Making wise use of that which others normally
would overlook or discard.

∽ **Responsibility vs. Unreliability**
Knowing and doing what is expected of you.

∽ **Reverence vs. Disrespect**
Being aware of God's authority and work in your life
through other people and events in your life.

∽ **Security vs. Anxiety**
Structuring your life around what is eternal and
cannot be destroyed or taken away.

∽ **Self-control vs. Self-indulgence**
Being free to choose a course of action over
impulse or emotion.

∽ **Sincerity vs. Hypocrisy**
Being eager to do what is right with transparent
motives.

∽ **Thoroughness vs. Incompleteness**
Knowing what factors will diminish the effective-
ness of work or words, if neglected.

∽ **Thriftiness vs. Extravagance**
Using money in a resourceful, prudent manner.

∽ **Tolerance vs. Prejudice**
Accepting others as unique expressions of specific
character qualities in varying degrees of maturity.

∽ **Truthfulness vs. Deception**
Earning future trust by accurately reporting facts.

∽ **Virtue vs. Impurity**
Pursuing moral excellence in all areas of life.

∽ **Wisdom vs. Natural Inclinations**

Seeing and responding to life situations from God's frame of reference.

List one or two of these traits that best characterize your loved one. Give an example of times when you witnessed these qualities in his or her life:

1. _____

_____

_____

_____

_____

_____

_____

_____

2. _____

_____

_____

_____

_____

_____

_____

_____

Chapter Four

Biographical and Personality Questions

This section is meant to help you gather two types of information: The biographical questions ask for basic information needed for a formal eulogy and newspaper notices; the personal questions are meant to invoke memories about the deceased that give clues as to who he/she really was. This process may help you decide which qualities and memories should be expressed in the service.

41

The object is not to answer all the questions. Respond only to those aspects that are unique to the deceased, and meaningful to the family. The family may wish to discuss these questions collectively. Not only can reminiscing together be part of the healing process, but as one person's memory triggers another's, more creative responses will probably result. You may want to record this discussion on cassette or on videotape as a keepsake.

Biographical Information:

1. Full Name _____ Nickname _____

2. Age____ Birthdate ____ Birthplace _____

3. Name of Spouse _____ Date Married_____

4. Children of this marriage (ages) _____
   _____
   _____

5. Children of previous marriage (ages) _____
   _____
   _____

6. Stepchildren (If so noted)_____
   _____
   _____

7. Mother, father_____
   _____

8. Brothers, sisters _____
   _____
   _____

9. Survived by (if different from above) _____

_____

_____

(Circle the names of any deceased in # 3–8.)

10. Education _____

_____

11. Employed by _____ # of years _____

12. Military Service _____ Dates _____

13. Church Affiliation _____

_____

Association with special groups, causes (Scouts, Little League, political groups etc.)

_____

14. What significant local or national events occurred during his or her lifetime? (For example, who was President? Was the country at war? Was he born during a blizzard? Or move his family from California after an earthquake? What was happening in his home town and/or the world at the time this person lived that would put his life in context?

Year of birth _____

_____

_____

_____

Childhood _____

_____

_____

_____

School Years _____

_____

_____

_____

College Years _____

_____

_____

_____

Marriage/Family _____

_____

_____

_____

Year of Death _____

_____

_____

_____

_____

Personal Information:

1. What is the best thing this person did for you? _____

_____

_____

_____

_____

_____

2. What's your favorite memory of him/her? _____

_____

_____

_____

3. What was his/her favorite song, poem (secular or religious), or Scripture passage? _____

_____

Do you know why? _____

_____

4. What hobbies did he/she have? _____
How did it reflect his/her approach to life? (i.e., para-chuting—thrill seeker, fishing—solitude, a thinker)

_____

_____

_____

5. What was his/her favorite object (something on a desk, a picture, a book, a clipping) that reflected something about him or her? (i.e., a favorite jacket, chair—enjoyed being surrounded by familiar things.) _____

_____

_____

_____

6. What were his/her favorite foods? _____

_____

_____

_____

7. Did he/she place a premium on tradition or on innovation? _____

    _____

    _____

8. What were some of his/her favorite expressions? _____

    _____

    _____

    _____

9. Why did you enjoy being around him/her? _____

    _____

    _____

    _____

10. What were his/her gifts? _____

    _____

    _____

11. What attitude would you say characterized his/her life?

    _____

    _____

    If negative, what from his/her background attributed to it?

    _____

    _____

    _____

    _____

    _____

12. In what ways did he/she overcome the limitations of his/her upbringing?_____

_____

_____

_____

13. What was his/her greatest struggle? _____

_____

_____

_____

14. What do you think was his/her greatest achievement?

_____

_____

15. What would he/she consider the greatest achievement?

_____

_____

_____

16. What was his/her greatest disappointment? _____

_____

_____

17. What gave him/her the most satisfaction? _____

_____

_____

_____

18. What was his/her outstanding character trait? _____

_____

Example _____

_____

_____

19. What is one thing you learned from him/her? _____

_____

_____

20. If he/she could say one thing at the service, what would it be? _____

_____

_____

_____

21. What would you say was his/her passion in life? _____

_____

_____

_____

22. How would he/she like to be remembered? _____

_____

_____

23. How is the world different because of his/her life? _____

_____

_____

_____

_____

Part Three:

*Planning
The Service*

To everything there is a season,
a time for every purpose under heaven.

—Ecclesiastes 3:1

Chapter Five

Elements of the Service

*B*efore exploring the more imaginative aspects of the funeral, we need to set up a framework for the service. The following order of service provides a basic format, but keep in mind that it is only a tool. Discard what does not fit and arrange the elements of the service in whatever way will best suit your purpose. A typical order of service could be:

Prelude
Special Music
Prayer
Sermon
Scripture Reading
Congregational Singing
Postlude
Eulogy/Creative Participation

This outline can be used simply as a fill-in-the-blank format, but personalizing the elements of the service creates the powerful memorial that will achieve the goals set for the service in Chapter One.

The eulogy/creative participation and music (special and congregational) sections will be discussed in detail later in the book. Still, the other elements of the service also provide unique opportunities to add impact to the parting.

Prelude and Postlude

The prelude and postlude are usually not considered part of the service itself. However, they can add a meaningful memory to the occasion. Begin by selecting pieces that were favorites of the loved one. In planning the service, family members often recall more than one or two songs that were favorites or had particular meaning to the deceased. There may not be time to use them all in the service, but they can be used in the prelude and postlude.

My husband, Joe, loves classical music and two of his favorite pieces, Pachelbel's "Canon in D" and Vivaldi's "Four Seasons," would be appropriate for the prelude. Of course, hiring an orchestra wouldn't be feasible, but most churches and funeral homes are equipped with a quality sound system that allows taped music to be used very effectively.

If there is a special significance to the music played in the prelude or postlude you may want to note it in the bulletin

Prayer and Scripture Reading

These can be done by the minister, or they can be opportunities to allow other people to participate in the service. If the selected Scripture passage had particular value to the deceased, it would denote what was important to him, and may give a clue as to what the theme for the service should be. Otherwise, the Scripture and prayer should relate to the overall focus.

Sermon

Even though you are not responsible to give the sermon, you may want to give some thought to the basic theme and discuss it with your minister. It's common for the eulogy to be a kind of sermon/eulogy combination. Whether or not the two are combined, each has a very specific and different function. The eulogy focuses on the person; the sermon turns the focus to God. I have devoted an entire chapter to the eulogy because I feel it offers great opportunity for creativity and is not necessarily given by a minister. The sermon, however, is usually given by the pastor of the deceased and/or his loved ones.

In the course of planning the funeral, it's important that the family communicate clearly to the pastor what focus the family would like the service to have. It could be hope, forgiveness, the lordship of Christ, worship, comfort, salvation, priorities, family, or a particular character trait of the deceased, such as humility, perseverance, or selflessness. If the minister knows what direction the family wants the service to take, it will be easier for him to give his words the same direction.

Up to this point, the elements of the service may seem to be loosely connected, but in his address to the congregation, the minister should be able to tie them together. He can state overtly what is being acted out in the course of the service.

Bulletin

Although not an element of the service per se, it is a very helpful tool for giving order and cohesiveness to the service. (See sample bulletin in Chapter Ten.) Because of the time crunch, people may feel it impractical to use a bulletin, but most churches now have some sort of desk-top publishing that would allow them to print a bulletin in-house. If yours does not, many quick print shops can print the bulletin in one day, especially if the circumstances are explained.

A printed bulletin allows the congregation to know where you are going in the service. Many things can be noted there that would otherwise go unsaid, such as an explanation of any symbols used and the names of people participating in the service. If desired, the relationship of these people to the deceased can be stated as well. Having a printed bulletin also gives people a keepsake to take away from the service.

The facts about the deceased's life may be stated in a brief paragraph in the bulletin rather than shared orally in the service. The facts are important and of interest, but the service time would probably be better spent in sharing the more personal aspects of your loved one's life.

Chapter Six

Who Does What?

When a death occurs, the first per-son most people call is a minister. Usually, the pastor, priest or rabbi plays a primary role in helping the family plan the funeral service and while most of the clergy see this as a prac-tical way to minister to their parishioners (and it is!), this role is often theirs by default.

Because of their closeness, family members usually are in the best position to share what was meaningful in the

deceased's life. Also, planning the service offers many therapeutic benefits for the bereaved. Not only does it gives them
the opportunity to give their memories concrete form and
expression, but the process itself can help them and others
deal with their loss.

Perhaps the impact of a deliberately planned ceremony
has never been more dramatically illustrated than at the
funeral of President John F. Kennedy. Upon returning to
Washington after her husband's assassination, Mrs.
Kennedy immediately dispatched an aide to research the
funeral procession of Abraham Lincoln. With that information, she then forged the classic farewell for her slain
husband. The horse drawn wagon carrying his flag draped
coffin...a riderless horse...the sound of horses' hooves
echoing down Pennsylvania Avenue while crowds watched
in silence...all created a powerful ritual of mourning. At that
moment, an historic tragedy and the anguish of personal
loss melded in a way that both comforted and united us.
"She taught us how to grieve," said one historian later of the
gift Jackie Kennedy gave to a nation of Americans. It's a gift
we, too, can give to others. True, a measure of courage is
required to pull oneself together and create a unique
memorial out of one's sorrow, but while it can be difficult, it
can also be very rewarding.

Not only does it seems fitting that those closest to the
deceased should have a hand in writing the final chapter of
his or her life, but sometimes the minister who personally
knew the deceased may not be available. The family should
know that funerals do not have to be conducted by a member of the clergy. Neither does the minister (or whoever is
asked to conduct the funeral) have to be the one who creates the service or gives the sermon or eulogy. If the
deceased did not know his pastor well, or had been particu-
larly close to someone who ministered to him before death,
it might be more meaningful for that person to lead the
memorial service. Usually, a pastor will try to discern how

much involvement the family wishes him to have in the planning and executing of the service, and will take his cue from them.

Some people wish to plan every last detail. Others feel strongly about one or two particular elements of the service and are relieved to have the minister take over the rest. Whatever your preference, communicate your wishes to your pastor early on, so that your expectations are clear.

If you do not wish to give up the privilege of planning a loved one's funeral, certain decisions must be made. Who should be responsible to plan the service? Who should execute and lead it? Who should give the eulogy? Who decides what creative expressions to use?

By rights, the responsibility for making funeral arrangements falls to the nearest of kin. Often the immediate family will want to meet together to discuss plans and what role each person will take. If the next of kin seems to need or want help in making arrangements, you may be able to suggest someone among the family or close friends who would be suited to assist. This person would be a service coordinator. Again, the pastor often assumes this role, but if the service will entail more than a standard format, it may require more time than a minister has time to give.

There is much to be said for having an objective person as a service coordinator. In times of crisis, people do not always think clearly, let alone convey their thoughts accurately to others. A service coordinator should be someone who, if necessary, could help the family sift through their thoughts and memories as they plan the service. This person should be well organized and sensitive to the needs of the family. The service coordinator's primary role is to handle the logistics of the service. (A detailed account of these responsibilities is given in Chapter Nine in the checklist for the service.)

It is likely the minister will be involved in planning and executing the service, even if the next of kin or the service coordinator takes responsibility for it. The pastor or priest may even be asked to carry out some of the specific duties. If so, it is important that he knows exactly what the family has planned, what he is expected to do, and what others will be doing. Chapter Ten contains a service outline to be used as the service is being planned—be sure your pastor gets a copy.

If the funeral is being held in a church and someone other than a minister at the church is asked to lead, be sure to clear your plans beforehand with the appropriate people to avoid any misunderstandings. This may include the church secretary, another staff person, or a committee member. It's a good idea to ask your pastor who needs to be informed.

The person to give the eulogy for the deceased may be: a friend; a significant person in his life (a teacher, co-worker, pastor); someone who had a unique place in his illness or death crisis (a nurse, doctor, therapist); someone whose life was touched by his life in a special way (perhaps a student); and of course, members of the family.

My father gave the eulogy at my mother's funeral. It seemed appropriate because of their special relationship. We felt that he, more than anyone else, could communicate the significance of my mother's presence in our lives. For him, it was an outlet for grief. For the family, it provided an invaluable memory of my mother's life from the perspective of my father's love for her.

If someone very close to the deceased is being asked to give the eulogy, don't press for an immediate response. Give them some time to think about it. At first, the emotional strain of giving the eulogy may seem too much, but many change their minds as the need to find some tangible way to express grief presses in on them.

If no one close to the family feels comfortable in giving the eulogy, a minister is a logical choice. He is experienced in handling such events and hopefully, he has had opportunity to share deeply with the deceased and the family during this and other crises. However, the eulogy, more than any other part of the service, provides the opportunity for significant people in the life of the deceased to honor him or her. There are many ways this can be done so that their unique perspective on their loved one's life can be acknowledged without the pressure of public speaking.

Part Four:

*Creative
Celebrations
of Life*

Cause me to hear Your lovingkindness
in the morning, for in You do I trust.
Cause me to know the way
in which I should walk,
for I lift up my soul to You.

—Psalm 143:8

Chapter Seven

Creative Eulogies, Rituals, and Symbols

From the beginning, Michael and Marie Lucey weren't given much hope—their twins, Jessica Michelle and Erin Elizabeth had been born prematurely. "It'll be a miracle if either one of them makes it," the doctor told them. Jessica lived only a few hours. So with his wife and other daughter still in the hospital, Michael gave this poetic eulogy at his youngest daughter's funeral. In it one hears not only a father's grief but triumph of the human spirit over death.

JESSICA MICHELLE LUCEY

I want to tell you something about Jessica. Who she was, what she did with her life, how she affected her world, her mother and father.

I didn't expect much from this little girl, and must admit that I didn't think of her as Jessica Michelle Lucey:
> *not as she grew within Marie,*
> *not when she was delivered,*
> *not even as she lay in Marie's arms.*

That's not to say I didn't love her. I most certainly did, as much as I loved any of my children.

But when Marie placed Jessica in my hands, I met my daughter. When I felt her move in her blanket, I learned about her. When I watched her cough, I learned some more. And Jessica began to teach me.

My first lesson was how much I love my daughters: how deeply that love runs, how completely it envelops me and my life; and maybe a necessary part of the lesson, how painful such complete love can be.

She was a darling little girl — Jessica. Cute, beautiful, pure—a tiny piece of Marie and me. I felt as though, in my hands, I held my own heart. I had what I needed so desperately, and if I lost it, I would be lost.

So I stood there and held my daughter, and let her lessons wash over me. I made no attempt to understand all the emotions that flowed through me, but just focused on this beautiful girl.

*I brought her to the window to show her day light,
and warned her of the cold when she was weighed.
We talked to her about her sisters and told her about
many of you. We sang to her a song we used to sing
Nicole to sleep.*

*There was nothing between my daughter and me,
nothing between Jessica and Marie—just one tiny
babe with her mother and father.*

*Unobstructed, Jessica plucked at reservoirs of emotion
we would normally keep hidden away. She touched
pools of love we held for our children that we would
have never discovered. And once touched by this
innocent little girl, these emotions were released—
waves of love mixed with pain, mixed with joy. All
of which she drank in quietly, comfortably.*

*And when she had her fill, she slipped back to the
Lord.*

*When Jessica Michelle finally left us, she left me a
tremendous feeling of peace. I felt complete. One of
her lessons began to take shape, began to focus in
front of me.*

*It occurred to me—what are we here for, if not for
each other? And what can we truly give to each other
beyond our attention, compassion and our love?*

*In a marriage, those gifts are included freely, and
both people are greater because of it. But it is the
giving that strengthens us, the giving that fills each
person with more gifts and the relationship grows.*

*How more perfect, then, is union between a mother
and her child, a father and his daughter. The child
has no obligation to give, only accept. We are bound
to give, and in giving, find those wells and springs of
love that can make us great.*

*When I cry today, the tears are for myself, for memo-
ries that I'll never create with my daughter, Jessica.
She lived a full life, my youngest girl. Her world was
the arms of her mother and the hands of her father,
and she left her world far better than she found it.
She accomplished in her seventy minutes what we
should all try to accomplish in our seventy years.*

*For today, there is for Marie and me, a thriving child
named Nicole Marie; a lovely courageous angel
named Erin Elizabeth; and chance that the Lord
may bless us with other children. In every case,
Jessica's lesson will live, having taken root in our
hearts.*

*And if my child is blind, I will be her eyes.
If she is deaf, I will be her ears.
I will be those things, not because she is my child.
I am those things—because I am hers.*

Michael Lucey's words brought hope and perspective
into what could have seemed a pointless tragedy and is a
powerful example of the impact a eulogy can have.

The word "eulogy" itself has several meanings. It can be
a commendatory formal statement, or it can mean "high
praise." What usually takes place in a funeral service is a
combination of these two—a formal oration giving high
praise to the deceased. If, however, we use the term in the
broader sense of giving high praise, the potential for creativity is greatly increased. This is important because often

people wish to participate in the parting, but feel unable to speak at the service.

It is not necessary to confine the eulogy to the formal speech. The acting out of rituals and the designation of symbols can also express the high value one attaches to a loved one and provide an emotional release for the mourners. Whether verbal or nonverbal, these ideas offer new possibilities for celebrating a life and participating in the parting:

- ∞ Read a loving memorial written by loved ones.

- ∞ Display drawings by children beside the casket or at the church entrance.

- ∞ Design the service bulletin cover, if there is time (a good opportunity for children).

- ∞ Ask for some form of participation from a club or group in which the deceased was active, such as a band, choir, Boy Scouts, etc. For example, a Boy Scout leader could have his boys stand guard behind the pallbearers. A choir could sing a favorite song.

- ∞ If he or she was a musician, play an audio or video tape of a performance.

- ∞ Create a slide or video presentation of the deceased using his favorite music as background. The family can write the narration, if desired, to be read by another.

- ∞ Compile a photo collage to display beside the casket or in the sanctuary. Use both old and new photographs.

∞ Ask several people to share vignettes of the life of the deceased. Perhaps each one could focus on a particular aspect of his life...work, family, friends, faith.

∞ Display a favorite object as a life symbol. For example, a little girl's music box. Have a family member explain why she loved it. How did it reflect her personality? This could be written by one person and read by another.

∞ Give people attending the service the opportunity to share spontaneously what the deceased meant in their lives. It may be wise to put a note in the bulletin saying this will be done so that people have time to gather their thoughts and composure. Also, be prepared for a few moments' silence. People are hesitant at first and it can take a while for them to summon the courage to speak. To help get things started, you may want to ask one or two people ahead of time. Once the barrier is broken, the problem is more likely to be limiting the number of participants, so you may want to begin by stating the time allotted for this part of the service.

∞ Ask people to complete a sentence such as...

"My favorite memory of Mary is...."
"The most meaningful words Mary spoke to
    me were...."
"The last time I saw Mary...."
"I remember Mary being happiest when...."
"The quality I most valued in Mary was...."

∞ Read something written by the deceased, such as a letter.

∞ Read a favorite poem, excerpt from a book or Bible passage, lines from a movie, or lyrics to a song. Share the significance of the words in the context of the life of the deceased.

∞ Re-create memories that were meaningful to the deceased. For example, have children or grandchildren sing or play songs that were sung on special occasions. It could be recorded or videotaped in advance if it would be too difficult to perform at the service.

∞ Use a candle to symbolize the life of the deceased. It can be lit at the beginning of the service and extinguished at the end after being joined with a larger candle. The candle ceremony, signifying a passing from one life to the next, can be carried out by a family member.

∞ Use objects such as jewelry as symbols of some aspect of the life of the deceased. The object can then be given to a loved one after the service.

The use of objects as symbols in the service can be very meaningful, especially when the life shared with one who has died was brief. Children who lose parents, or parents who lose a child, do not have a lifetime of memories to sustain them. Marie bought a *mizpah* charm when Jessica died. She engraved the twin's birth dates on it and pinned half onto the little blanket Jessica was buried with. The other half was for her sister, Erin. When Erin died several weeks later, Marie kept the second half of the charm for herself. "I wore it for at least a year," she said, "and people would ask, 'who has the other half?' It gave me an opportunity, at least once a day, to tell someone about the twins and I needed to do that. I had lost two children others hadn't met and I wanted them to remember that Jessica and Erin had lived. They were and still are part of our family."

An object will hold a different significance for each person. For you it may represent hope or be a source of comfort. Perhaps for another, like Marie, it will provide a natural opportunity to express grief. However they are used, symbols stir powerful memories we may draw on for a lifetime.

Chapter Eight

Music

Music has the potential to have a great impact upon those who attend the memorial service. It can be used creatively to accomplish any or all of several important goals:

- *to reflect the personality of the deceased.*
- *to convey the life message of the service.*
- *to communicate compassion and comfort to family and friends.*

- ∾ to give the opportunity of participation in the parting for someone special to the family or the deceased.

- ∾ to direct the congregation toward God through thanksgiving and worship.

I attended a friend's funeral where two very untraditional songs were used. The first was "America, the Beautiful," chosen because my friend was a fierce patriot. Al's conversation was always seasoned with stories of his World War II days. Yet he was a gentle, peace-loving man and his tales never glorified the horror of war. Al's stories were mostly about the funny things that happened as people from different cultures and backgrounds interacted while fighting together for a cause they believed in.

Al loved America, valued her freedom, and gladly took his place to defend it. "America the Beautiful" accurately reflected the patriotism that held a high priority in his life. It suited him perfectly.

Al's service concluded with one of his favorite songs, "Lord of the Dance." I found myself greatly moved as the happy melody of this hymn celebrated the resurrection of Christ. This was not the end for Al Nosenzo. Nor was grief the end for his wife, Betty, or his friends who loved him. Strength came from the conviction that Jesus is Lord, and that one day, even death must give way to the One who is "Lord of the Dance." It was an uplifting way to conclude the memorial of a very special man.

There are many ways music can help us participate in the parting. It's okay to be untraditional. It may even be appropriate to use secular and Christian music together. My sister and her husband, Ray, have preplanned their funerals. At Ray's service, since they want people to participate in the things Ray most enjoys in life, they've planned a half-hour, informal prelude complete with a family sing-a-long and surfer music.

Some people might think surfer music is going a bit too far, but anyone who knows Ray would understand. It represents many memories of the man as well as the good times he shared with family and friends. He loves the ocean and surfer music has been part of their family's fun times for years. Having the nontraditional part of the service beforehand will give people the option to be part of the more intimate memorial, if they wish, but will not detract from the service that follows.

There are certain songs we think of as being traditionally used at funerals, but the first song that comes to mind is not always the most meaningful. Traditional songs are often used because thinking of other options can be intimidating. However, with some thought and effort, it is possible to find music that not only expresses the theme of the service, but holds special significance to the family as well. We may discover it through family discussions, or perhaps by leafing through a songbook used in regular worship, or going through the tape and CD collections of the deceased. Just seeing a title may remind us of a special time and place in his spiritual journey, or scanning a list will bring to mind another song or chorus that fits the occasion.

In the case of sudden death, it's doubtful that the family would have time to track down hymns and choruses they'd like to use. Too often, a loved song must be omitted from the service because it can't be located. So where there is time to preplan the funeral, it's important to gather both the words and music to all songs you may want to use.

The following section is intended to be a resource and a catalyst for further thought, not a comprehensive list. Music selected for the funeral tends to be effective to the degree that it reflects the personality and life's mission of the deceased. Some of the following songs and hymns would not be considered traditional funeral music, but all evoke strong themes that may make them appropriate for a memorial service.

Traditional and Gospel Hymns

Taken from *Great Hymns of the Faith* (Singspiration/ Zondervan)

The Lordship of Christ

Jesus Shall Reign
Turn Your Eyes Upon Jesus
O Worship the King
Love Divine
Sing Praise to God Who Reigns Above
Come Thou Almighty King
Praise Ye the Lord the Almighty
The Lord Is King
I Sing the Mighty Power of God
This Is My Father's World
Crown Him with Many Crowns
Rejoice—the Lord Is King!

Comfort

A Mighty Fortress Is Our God
Great Is Thy Faithfulness
The Great Physician
O the Deep, Deep Love of Jesus
May Jesus Christ Be Praised
Sun of My Soul
O Come, O Come, Emmanuel
Rock of Ages
Christ the Lord Is Risen Today
Holy Ghost, with Light Divine
Spirit of God, Descend Upon My Heart
O Love That Wilt Not Let Me Go
In Times Like These
He Hideth My Soul
A Shelter in the Time of Storm
Hiding in Thee
What a Friend We Have in Jesus

Peace

Like a River Glorious
Wonderful Peace
Be Still, My Soul
Guide Me, O Thou Great Jehovah

Care

Savior, Like a Shepherd Lead Us
Standing on the Promises
He Leadeth Me
All the Way My Savior Leads Me
God Leads Us Along
Day by Day
I Need Thee Every Hour
It's Just Like His Great Love

Assurance of Salvation

And Can It Be That I Should Gain?
Wonderful Grace of Jesus
I Know Whom I Have Believed
My Faith Has Found a Resting Place
Amazing Grace
Blessed Assurance
It Is Well with My Soul
How Firm a Foundation
The Solid Rock
Leaning on the Everlasting Arms

Praise

O For a Thousand Tongues
Fairest Lord Jesus
More Love to Thee

My Jesus, I Love Thee
Praise Him! Praise Him!
To God Be the Glory
God of Our Fathers
How Great Thou Art

Hope of Reuniting

Blest Be the Tie That Binds
Sweet By and By
O That Will Be Glory
For All the Saints
Shall We Gather at the River

Choruses and Contemporary Music

Hundreds of wonderful praise choruses and contemporary songs can be appropriate for memorial services. If you want a particular song but are unable to find words and/or music through your local church, the resources mentioned below are a good place to start. The titles under each source reflect the style of the choruses found in each.

The *Hosanna Songbook* series by Integrity Music is an excellent resource. Used in a wide cross-section of churches, these series are readily available in most Christian bookstores. There are tapes, CDs, and written music for each set. The songbooks have multiple indexes listing songs according to topics and Scripture references making it easy to find appropriate songs.

North American Liturgy Resources (NALR) publishes *Glory and Praise,* a multi-volume series (with topical and scriptural indexes) containing songs more frequently used in the Catholic and Episcopal churches. Many of these songs have been compiled in smaller editions (such as *Gentle Night*), and have companion tapes and CDs. These materials are not always on the local Christian bookstore shelves, but they can easily be ordered.

Songs of Praise (Servant Music) and *Scripture in Song* (Benson Co.) also are good resources for familiar choruses.

Hosanna Music Songbook 6

There Is None Like You
Sure Foundation
The Lord Is My Light
Under the Shadow
Join Our Hearts
Rock of Ages
Be Glorified

Glory and Praise, Vol. 3

By Name I Have Called You
God Is So Good
May We Praise You
Only This I Want
This Alone

Gentle Night

Just Begun
Let the Valleys Be Raised
A Time Will Come for Singing

From Songs of Praise (Servant Music)

This Is the Day*
How Great Is Our God
I Am the Bread of Life
They that Wait Upon the Lord
Glorify Thy Name**
I Am the Resurrection
He Is Lord*
You Are Near
The Prayer of St. Francis*

From Scripture in Song I

His Loving Kindness
Praise the Name of Jesus
I Will Enter His Gates with Thanksgiving
The Lord Liveth
Jehovah Jireh
Bind Us Together
Our God Reigns
Something Beautiful

From Scripture in Song II

Majesty
Jesus, Name Above All Names
The Lord Is My Light

* Also in Scripture in Song I
** Also in Scripture in Song II

Miscellaneous Sources

My Father's Eyes (Gary Chapman/Paragon Music Corp)
Arms of Love (Amy Grant/Bug & Bear Music & Meadowgreen)
Do I Trust You (Twila Paris/Singspiration)
Friend of a Wounded Heart (Claire Cloninger and
          Wayne Watson/Word)
The Lord Is My Shepherd (Melody and Keith Green/Birdwing)
Make My Life a Prayer to You (Melody Green/April Music)
The Lord Is So Good (Marty Goetz/In the Reign Music)
Raining on the Inside (Kathy Troccoli and Amy Grant/Bug & Bear
          Music & Meadowgreen)
Doubly Good (Richard Mullins/Meadowgreen)
Household of Faith (Brent Lamb & John Rosasco/Benson Company)
The Lord Is My Light and My Salvation (Maranatha)

Part Five:

Writing It Down

So teach us to number our days,
that we may gain a heart of wisdom.

—Psalm 90:12

Chapter Nine

Memorial Service Checklist

he Memorial Service Checklist is simply an organizational tool to remind you of the specific arrangements that need to be made. Any responsibilities the family wishes to take over should be noted. The remaining preparations can be made by the minister or the service coordinator.

Memorial Service Checklist

Memorial Service For _____

Date of Service _____

Place _____

Time _____

Officiating Minister _____

❑ Select Service Coordinator, if desired.

❑ Service Coordinator

❑ Contact minister.

❑ Confirm arrangements for church or facilities.

❑ Arrange for Pallbearers, if needed:

1. _____ 2. _____

3. _____ 4. _____

5. _____ 6. _____

❑ Contact whoever will be giving eulogy:

_____

❑ Contact musicians:

❑ Organist _____

❑ Pianist _____

❑ Vocalist _____

❑ Other vocalists/instrumentalists _____

_____

❑ Sound technician, if needed _____

❏ Arrange for taping or video of service, if desired.

❏ Arrange for typing and printing of bulletin, if used.

   ❏ Typist _____

   ❏ Printer _____

❏ Bring objects or symbols to be used during the
service.

❏ Coordinate service with minister.

   ❏ Give minister a copy of the checklist (note
which items you would like him to arrange).

   ❏ Give minister a copy of the service planner.

Chapter Ten

Memorial Service Planner and Bulletin

The Memorial Service Planner notes the person(s) who will be participating in each part of the service. Fill in the parts you wish to plan, and strike out any section you wish to delete. The remainder can be completed by the service coordinator or minister. The order of service will be drawn up from the information on this sheet.

Memorial Service Planner

Prelude: Played by _____

                    Special Requests _____

                    _____

                    _____

                    Time allotted _____

Opening Prayer: Given by _____

Music:

           Congregational Songs:

             # _____   _____

             # _____   _____

             # _____   _____

           Special Music:

           _____ Sung by _____

           _____ Sung by _____

Scripture Reading:

                    Read by _____

Eulogy: Given by _____

                    Special use of objects or symbols _____

                    _____

                    _____

                    Explained by _____

Letters, tapes, slides, or videos _____

_____

_____

_____

Read or narrated by _____

Sermon: Given by _____

Theme _____

Closing Prayer: Given by _____

Postlude: Played by _____

Special Requests _____

_____

_____

_____

_____

_____

IN MEMORY OF
JONATHAN ELLIS MARTIN

A service of celebration and thanksgiving.

Whatever you do in word or deed, do all in the name of the Lord Jesus,
giving thanks to God the Father through him.   Colossians 3:17

Prelude
          A selection of Jonathan's favorite hymns and choruses

Candle Lighting

Address and prayer   Pastor Freidman

Hymn #13"   Praise Ye the Lord the Almighty"   Congregation

Eulogy - Expressions of gratitude by his loved ones
          Joseph Bartello—Co-worker
          Andrew Seamond—Friend
          Letter by Joan Martin—Wife

"Praise the Name of Jesus"   See Insert   Congregation
"Something Beautiful"

Scripture Reading   Psalm 84   Jason Smith

Sermon   Pastor Stevens

"Bless the Lord, O My Soul"   Ensemble

Prayer   Pastor Stevens

"A Mighty Fortress Is Our God"   Congregation

Candle Ceremony   Alex Martin
          The solitary candle represents Jonathan's life. At the end of the
          service it will be used to light the new, unlit candle in the can-
          delabra. As the old one is extinguished, we acknowledge that
          Jonathan's home is now with God.

Pianist: Anna Marie Sanchez   Organist: Celia Brandt

JONATHAN ELLIS MARTIN

February 11, 1940 - December 6, 1989

Jonathan was born in San Francisco, California, where he resided for the first eighteen years of his life. In 1960, he moved to Long Beach, California to attend college. It was there he met his wife, Joan, whom he married in 1962. After graduating from college, Jonathan taught high school, and eventually became principal of Pacific High School in Seal Beach.

He was always involved with people—especially kids. As he supported his own three boys through numerous sports, he often included other kids who needed a relationship with a caring adult. Two of his pallbearers are boys he coached in Babe Ruth baseball.

At church, Jon was known for his warm smile and beautiful bass voice. He was a faithful, enthusiastic member of the mixed ensemble that is singing today in his honor.

Jonathan is survived by his wife, Joan; his sons, Steven, 23; Bryan, 22; and Alex, 15; his mother, Eileen Martin; and two sisters, Janice Walker and Joy Milano.

Part Six:

Planning Your Own Service

*Surely goodness and mercy
shall follow me all the days of my life
and I will dwell in the house
of the Lord forever.*

—Psalm 23:6

Chapter Eleven

Participating in Your Parting

*T*he primary motivation for planning one's own memorial service is to convey a specific message to those left behind.

In our parting, we wish to make a statement about our lives…we want our loved ones to know that our concern for them transcends death…we want to be assured that what has been important to us in life is communicated clearly at our death.

When we plan another's funeral, our desire is to honor his or her life. But when we plan our own, our intention is to affirm our life's purpose. A modification of the goals of a creative memorial service, given in Chapter One, reflects this difference.

The objectives in arranging our own parting are:

∞ To celebrate the principles and people we most value.

∞ To allow others to express their grief through participation in the service.

∞ To facilitate forgiveness and reconciliation.

∞ To direct our loved ones toward our hope in God.

The focus of the service will shift from what others can say about us to what we can impart to them. The service should provide an opportunity for our family and friends to express their feelings, but it also represents an opportunity for us. While we are yet living, we can find great satisfaction in knowing that our deepest emotions and values will be affirmed at our parting.

For this to happen, it's imperative to get our thoughts into a concrete form. Make it as simple or complex as you like. A pastor friend of mine intends to videotape his own sermon, but you may wish to simply write a letter or make an audio tape.

What actually occurs is a kind of give and take...a mutual participating in the parting ceremony. And what a comfort to know that you can have an impact on your family and friends through the words and rituals you plan for that day.

If you cannot identify the main themes of your life, the biographical and personal questions asked in Chapter Four may help. Though designed for another person to explore, going through this written process yourself may reveal patterns you have not yet recognized. You may want a close friend or relative to work through it with you.

Chapters Five through Eight will be helpful to you in thinking of creative ways to express your life's message. Complete the Memorial Service Checklist and the Service Planner given in Chapters Nine and Ten with whatever details are important to you.

Don't assume that any of your wishes are known. As a friend and I were discussing her funeral arrangements, I asked where she would want her memorial service held. She and her family had moved from their small home town to our area three years earlier. "I'd want the funeral here, of course," she replied.

"Does your husband know that?" I asked.

She thought carefully and said, "I don't think I ever mentioned it. I just assumed he'd know."

Whatever matters to you should be put in writing. The forms in this book are to help you think through the things that are important to you, and to make it easy for you to note them.

Once your plans are made, put them in a marked envelope and give them to whoever will be responsible for making your funeral arrangements. As a precaution, make a second copy to be filed elsewhere. I keep one on file at home, and my husband keeps a copy at his office.

You may want to keep your plans with your will, but remember that people seldom refer to the will immediately after death. The one place you *don't* want to put your plans is in a safe deposit box. They are usually sealed immediately upon the death of the signee and can't be opened until released by the court.

Finally, be sure several people know where your plans are kept. You want them to be found before, not after, your funeral.

Like a will, your plans should be updated from time to time. As your children become older, different memories or symbols may be more appropriate than what you planned when they were little. Also, as new people enter your life and your circumstances change, you will want your service to reflect your current relationships and situation.

One important benefit of planning your own memorial service is that in doing so, you cannot help but reflect on your life. Death gives us a perspective we need to consider far more often than we do. As we realize that our time with our loved ones is limited, we can seize the chance to restore broken relationships and to encourage those who have brought meaning to our lives.

It has often been said that funerals are not for the dead, but for the living. While this is very true, it is still possible for our funeral to have an impact on our own lives as well as the lives of those who will carry on after we are gone. The process of planning your own memorial service may prompt you to address relationships that need to be tended today. Now, while you are living, is the time to express the deep appreciation you feel for those you love.

As you think about who and what is important in your life, write the note that needs to be written. Make the phone call that should be made. Build on your faith. Speak words of encouragement to your family and friends.

The best parting is one which can be marked by celebration rather than regrets. Let the awareness of your mortality enhance your love for life and for those God has given you to share it. Let it fill you with gratitude for the gift of each day and motivate you to commit yourself fully to those things that will last an eternity.

A Note
From the Author...

A book like this one tends to raise as many questions as it answers. If there are certain aspects of death and dying you want to explore more fully, there are many excellent books on the subject. Billy Graham's book *Death and the Life After* is a great resource for those who are asking universal questions about death: What happens when we die? Is there a heaven and hell? How can we find peace in the midst of suffering?

Families making painful choices about life prolonging measures will find a sensitive exploration of this issue in John Sherrill's book *Mother's Song*. *Last Touch*, by Marilyn R. Becker, is a narrative guide for preparing for a parent's death and is especially helpful if you are caring for a dying loved one. *A Family's Guide to Death and Dying*, by Jim Towns, offers detailed instructions for handling the logistics of terminal illness and final arrangements.

If you need to understand what a dying person is feeling, *On Death and Dying* by Elizabeth Kubler-Ross, explains the coping mechanisms of the terminally ill. But the tasks of grieving fall to the living as well as the dying and much is now being written on this subject. Several authors, well respected in the area of grief work, are Harriet Schiff, Earl Grollman, and Judy Tatelbaum. But if a full sized book seems overwhelming, *Overcoming Loss: A Healing Guide*, by Dr. Rita Freedman, is a gentle opener. Short and simple, this small specialty book gives a good overview of facets of grief. A broader perspective is found in *Necessary Losses*, by Judith

Voirst which deals with the losses of each phase of life, including death.

If death has caused you to question your faith, *The Problem of Pain*, and *A Grief Observed*, by C.S. Lewis as well as Philip Yancey's book, *Disappointment with God*, can help you find firm theological ground in your sorrow.

For those of you who wonder if anyone has experienced the pain you feel yet survived, *To Live Again* by Catherine Marshall and *God In The Dark*, by Luci Shaw are two beautiful classic journals of grief, courage and comfort.

One daunting task we often face during bereavement is meeting the emotional needs of hurting children. However, books such as *About Dying* by Sarah Stein, can give you direction. This book with photographs, a simple text for children and an accompanying text for adults, is outstanding. Your local library also holds a rich supply of books to help you learn how to give a child permission to grieve. To find them, check the "Death and Dying" section (Dewey decimal number 155.937) in the adult section of the library. Books by Eda LeShan, Sarah Stein or Earl Grollman are a good place to start. One excellent guide for parents is *How Do We Tell the Children?* by Dan Schaefer and Christine Lyons. The book's layout, including the identification of common concerns of children by age, makes its insights and crisis-intervention strategies both clear and practical. Books written for children are usually shelved under the same Dewey decimal number but in the children's section. Along side books about death are many that deal with specific situations such as losing a brother or parent. These resources are invaluable to parents and friends who are at a loss about what a grieving child needs to hear and express.

Finally, there are times when books are not enough and we long for contact with another person who understands. Numerous support and self-help groups exist just for that purpose. Two organizations that have been very successful at providing a network for grieving people are the National

Hospice Organization and The Self-Help Center. Hospice is best known for its work with terminally ill patients and their families. The Self-Help Center is a clearing house organization that helps people link up with appropriate support groups. (For a more comprehensive list, see Towns' book, *A Family Guide to Death and Dying*.)

Dealing with death is often life's ultimate challenge. It's not, however, a challenge we were meant to face alone. Wherever you are in the journey, I pray that you will find comfort in God and the family and friends he's given you.

Resources

Organizations

National Hospice Organization
1901 North Moore Street #901
Arlington, VA 22209
(703) 234-5900

The Self-Help Center
1600 Dodge Avenue Suite S-122
Evanston, IL 60204
(312) 218-0470

Books for Adults

Becker, Marilyn R. *Last Touch.*
  Oakland, California: New Harbinger Publications, Inc., 1992.
Freedman, Dr. Rita. *Overcoming Loss: A Healing Guide.*
  White Plains: Peter Pauper Press, Inc., 1995
Graham, Billy. *Death and the Life After.*
  Dallas, Texas: Word Publishing, 1987
Grollman, Earl A. *Concerning Death, A Practical Guide for the Living.*
  Boston: Beacon Press, 1974
Grollman, Earl A. *When Your Loved One is Dying.*
  Boston: Beacon Press, 1980
Kubler-Ross, Elizabeth. *On Death and Dying.*
  New York: Macmillan, Collier Books, 1982.
Lewis, C.S. *A Grief Observed.* New York: Seabury Press, 1961.
Lewis, C.S. *The Problem of Pain.* New York: Macmillan, 1962.
Marshall, Catherine. *To Live Again.*
  Lincoln, Virginia: Chosen Books, 1957.
Schiff, Harriet. *Living Through Mourning: Finding Comfort and Hope when A Loved One Has Died.* New York: Viking, 1986

Schiff, Harriet. *The Bereaved Parent.* New York: Crown Publishers, 1977
Shaw, Lucy. *God in the Dark.*
        Grand Rapids, Michigan: Zondervan (Broadmoor Books), 1989.
Sherrill, John. *Mother's Song.* Lincoln, Virginia. Chosen Books, 1982
Tatelbaum, Judy. *The Courage to Grieve.*
        New York: Lippincott and Crowell, 1980
Towns, Jim. A Family *Guide to Death and Dying.*
        Wheaton, Illinois: Tyndale House, 1987.
Voirst, Judith. *Necessary Losses.* New York: Ballantine Books, 1986.
Yancy, Phillip. *Disappointment with God.* New York: Harper Collins, 1988.

Books for Children

Cohn, Janice. *I Had A Friend Named Peter.* New York: William Morrow and
        Company, Inc., 1987.
Greenlee, Sharon. *When Someone Dies.*
        Atlanta: Peachtree Publishers, 1993.
Grollman, Earl *A. Straight Talk About Death for Teenagers.*
        Boston: Beacon Press, 1993.
Grollman, Earl A. *Talking About Death: A Dialogue Between Parent and
        Child.* Boston: Beacon Press, 1976.
Hickman, Martha Whitmore. *Last Week My Brother Anthony Died.*
        Nashville: Abingdon Press, 1984.
LeShan, Eda. *Learning to Say Good-by.* New York: Macmillan, 1976.
Rofes, Eric E. *Kid's Book About Death and Dying.*
        Boston: Little, Brown, 1985.
Schaefer, Dan and Lyons, Christine. *How Do We Tell the Children?*
        New York: New Market Press, 1986.
Stein, Sarah. *About Dying.* New York: Walker, 1976.

Order Form

I would like to order *The Parting*.

Number of copies	@ $8.99 =	$ _____
($9.99 in Canada)		
Sales Tax (Georgia only)		$ _____

Shipping & Handling

To One Address	U.S. $3.00	$ _____
	Canada $4.00	$ _____
For each additional book add:		
	U.S. $1.00	$ _____
	Canada $1.50	$ _____

Total Order: $ _____

(Allow 4 – 6 wks for delivery. Satisfaction unconditionally guaranteed.)

To Order

Please fill out the information below and send with your remittance.
Prepayment required.
I am paying by: ❏ Check   ❏ Money Order
Name_____ Phone (___)_____
Organization _____
Address _____ City _____
State_____ Zip_____County_____

Mail To:

Jordan West Publications
Building B-9, Suite 547
2880 Holcomb Bridge Road
Alpharetta, GA 30202